Facilitator's Guide

THE Moral Imperative OF SCHOOL LEADERSHIP

Michael Fullan

CORWIN PRESS
A Sage Publications Company
Thousand Oaks, California

For information:

Corwin Press
A Sage Publications Company
2455 Teller Road
Thousand Oaks, California 91320
www.corwinpress.com

Sage Publications Ltd.
1 Oliver's Yard
55 City Road
London EC1Y 1SP
United Kingdom

Sage Publications India Pvt. Ltd.
B-42, Panchsheel Enclave
Post Box 4109
New Delhi 110 017 India

Library of Congress Cataloging-in-Publication Data

Fullan, Michael.
Facilitator's guide to The moral imperative of school leadership /
Michael Fullan.
        p. cm.
Includes bibliographical references.
ISBN 1-4129-1477-9
    1. School principals—Professional ethics. 2. Educational leadership—Moral and ethical aspects. 3. School principals—Inservice training. I. Fullan, Michael.
Moral imperative of school leadership. II. Title.
LB2831.9.F84 2005
371.2'012—dc22

                                        2004021691

04   05   06   07   10   9   8   7   6   5   4   3   2   1

Acquisitions Editor:	Robert D. Clouse
Editorial Assistant:	Jingle Vea
Production Editor:	Melanie Birdsall
Typesetter:	C&M Digitals (P) Ltd.
Cover Designer:	Lisa Miller

Contents

About the Author

 **Michael Fullan** is the former Dean of the Ontario Institute for Studies in Education of the University of Toronto. He is recognized as an international authority on education reform. He is engaged in training in, consulting for, and evaluating change projects around the world. His ideas for managing change are used in many countries, and his books have been published in several languages. His books, which are widely acclaimed, include the *What's Worth Fighting For* trilogy (with Andy Hargreaves), the *Change Forces* trilogy, *The New Meaning of Educational Change,* and *Leading in a Culture of Change* that was awarded the 2002 Book of the Year Award by the National Staff Development Council. His latest books are *Change Forces With a Vengeance,* completing the *Change Forces* trilogy, and *The Moral Imperative of School Leadership.* In April 2004, he was appointed Special Adviser on Education to the Premier, and Minister of Education in Ontario.

Introduction

This facilitator's guide is a companion for *The Moral Imperative of School Leadership* by Michael Fullan. It is designed to accompany the study of the book and provide assistance to group facilitators, such as school leaders, professional development coordinators, peer coaches, team leaders, mentors, and professors. Along with a summary of each chapter in the book, Michael Fullan has provided chapter discussion questions, activities, journal writing prompts, and suggestions for practical application.

Corwin Press also offers a free 16-page resource entitled *Tips for Facilitators* which includes practical strategies and tips for guiding a successful meeting. The information in this resource describes different professional development opportunities, the principles of effective professional development, some characteristics of an effective facilitator, the responsibilities of the facilitator, and useful ideas for powerful staff development. *Tips for Facilitators* is available for free download at the Corwin Press Web site (www.corwinpress.com, under "Extras").

How to Use the Guide

When using the guide during independent study, focus on the summaries and discussion questions.

For small study groups, the facilitator should guide the group through the chapter work.

For small or large group workshops, the facilitator should create an agenda by selecting activities and discussion starters from the chapter reviews that meet the group's goals, and guide the group through the learning process.

We recommend that facilitators download a copy of *Tips for Facilitators* and review the characteristics and responsibilities of facilitators and professional development strategies for different types of work groups and settings.

Chapter-By-Chapter Study Guide for *The Moral Imperative of School Leadership* by Michael Fullan

Discussion Questions

1. As a school leader, what goals would you like to accomplish?

2. What is school leadership? Who are school leaders?

3. What is system transformation? What should the new system look like?

4. How can principals and other school leaders assist in system transformation?

5. What drives you to want to make a difference in the system?

6. What conditions need to be present to affect powerful change in the system?

7. What do you expect from this book (or workshop)?

Chapter 1: Changing the Context

- It is the moral imperative of school leaders to change the context of public education. To begin changing the context, leaders must change their immediate situation. If one can change the thinking and the environment of school leaders, the system will follow.

- Change naturally produces anxiety and tension. A leader must create an environment conducive to change—a safe, open, and nurturing environment.

- The public education system impacts every individual in a democratic society, as parents, business owners, and citizens. Therefore, the public education system must be morally responsible for the academic achievement and personal and social development of all students. In its present state, the system is not meeting those responsibilities. In order to change the school system, principals and other school leaders must lead the charge by changing their schools and the system.

- The school principal is the pivotal leader working to guide and support dedicated teachers to "informed professional judgment" (Barber, 2002). Informed professional judgment looks like this:

    Colleagues working together to pursue deeper knowledge

    Interaction of peers inside and outside of their own schools

    Disciplined inquiry based on solid data

    Driven by a solid moral purpose

    Conducted by committed, disciplined teachers

- To ensure success, school leaders must create and sustain dedicated, morally committed, disciplined teachers. To accomplish this task, principals must attain Level 5 leadership:

    Have personal humility and professional will

    Find the right people, put them in the right positions, and then figure out where to go

    Remain absolutely certain that you will succeed, while honestly confronting the brutal facts of your reality

    Be clear about your passion, ability, and motives

    Create a culture of disciplined people, disciplined thought, and disciplined action

    Apply technology to support change

- To affect significant change in the public education system, there must be more Level 5 leaders. Principals must act more like chief operating officers than managers.

Discussion Questions

1. What is the role of public education in a democratic society?

2. In what way does the failure or success of the public education system affect society?

3. What is your role as a school leader in affecting change in society?

4. Fullan believes "both academic achievement and personal and social development are core purposes of the public school system." Do you agree or disagree? Why?

5. Compare and contrast informed professional judgment with the practices in most schools. What forms the basis for informed professional judgment? How can more schools move in that direction?

6. What does a principal as COO look like? What qualities or characteristics would he or she possess? How would he or she behave? What strategies does he or she utilize to guide the school to success?

Activities

● *Informed Professional Judgment*

Time: 30 minutes

Materials: Chart paper, markers, masking tape, *The Moral Imperative of School Leadership* by Michael Fullan

Refer to the discussion of Michael Barber's study on page 6. If participants have not already read the selection, ask them to read it silently or in small groups.

Divide the room into four imaginary quadrants. Post a piece of chart paper on each wall and label each quadrant with one of the four conditions Barber describes: uninformed professional judgment, uninformed prescription, informed prescription, informed professional judgment. Then start a brief discussion to define each condition. As a visual reminder, write the key criteria on the chart paper in each quadrant.

Ask participants to stand up and move to the quadrant they feel most closely describes their current situation. Allow a couple of minutes for people to move around and then facilitate an analysis of the results. Ask questions such as, where do most schools fall and why do you think most schools fall in this category?

Initiate a conversation between participants in opposing quadrants. Encourage them to discuss what is working for them and what needs improvement to achieve the desired "informed professional judgment." Bring the group back together to discover how this book will help them on their journey.

● *Acting as a Level 5 Leader*

Time: 1 hour

Materials: A visual of Jim Collins's leadership hierarchy (p. 10), *The Moral Imperative of School Leadership* by Michael Fullan

Prepare a visual of Jim Collins's five-level leadership hierarchy. You can make an overhead transparency, a handout, or a digital representation.

If necessary, generate a brief discussion about the qualities of a leader at each level of the hierarchy. Ask participants to think about what a leader at each level looks like in a real-life setting on a daily basis.

Organize the participants into pairs or small groups and assign a level of the hierarchy to each group. Ask them to develop a short role-play to demonstrate how a leader on that level would handle a particular situation that occurs on a typical school day. You can suggest a common scenario or prompt groups to determine their own.

Encourage the groups to perform the role-play in front of all the participants. Then discuss the positive aspects of each level. Guide the discussion to include insights for how to achieve the higher levels of the leadership hierarchy.

Journal Writing

At what level of the leadership hierarchy do you define yourself at the present time? What level would you like to be? How can you get there?

Practical Application

Choose one characteristic from Collins's leadership hierarchy to which you aspire and incorporate it into your daily professional life. For example, making your vision clear and compelling. How will you incorporate that into your daily interactions with school personnel and system leaders? Record your thoughts and actions in your journal. Assess the effects of your new behavior on changing the context.

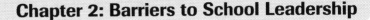

Chapter 2: Barriers to School Leadership

- There are two types of barriers to effective school leadership: self-imposed and system-imposed.

Self-Imposed Barriers

Perceived Limitations. Principals tend to play it safe for various reasons: teachers don't want to change, principal is not well-prepared for tasks and withdraws in the face of resistance, principal anticipates challenges from the system, principal is not well-informed of the system, the system tolerates inactivity from principals.

If-Only Dependency. In our complex society it is easy for principals to lose, or fail to gain, momentum by getting mired in the "if-onlys." If-only dependent leaders blame the system's inadequacies for the school's failures. "If only we had more funding for X, we would raise our test scores." Transcending the if-only thinking helps begin changing the system because the actions you take will change the context in which you work.

Loss of One's Moral Compass. It is easy for principals to lose their sense of purpose in the face of work overload and prolific expectations. When the moral compass is not set in the proper direction, the leadership position is filled with emptiness.

Not Taking Charge of One's Own Learning. School leaders must show others the importance of professional learning and development. They must continue to learn, inside and outside of the school, in order to provide positive change despite the obstacles inherent in the system.

The Responsibility Virus. The virus, described by Roger Martin (2002), has two strains: overresponsibility and underresponsibility. In any problem-solving situation humans will make very quick and unspoken statements. One person will take charge and the other will retreat. These reactions escalate and the passive one retreats further and the one in charge fills the void.

Principals are in a unique position and are affected by both strains of the virus. Many principals take on too much responsibility at their school site, while assuming too little responsibility in district or state policy.

System-Imposed Barriers

Centralization/Decentralization. Overcentralization results in overcontrol; decentralization results in chaos. The system fails to recognize the important role of the principal in mediating the state forces in solving local problems.

Role Overload and Role Ambiguity. The enormous amount of work and the ambiguous messages about the role of the principal hinders effective leadership and discourages quality candidates from entering the profession.

Limited Investment in Leadership Development. The system does not support adequate leadership development within the principalship or the school leadership team. School leadership must be distributed among the many levels of the school for the principal to be effective.

Neglect of Leadership Succession. The system often replaces leaders with the most convenient choice or a high-profile leader who is expected to provide "miracle cures."

However, what happens after the leader departs is often a more accurate assessment of his or her success than what was accomplished during his or her tenure. The effective leader leaves behind a legacy of other effective leaders who are committed to carrying on and going even deeper.

Absence of a System Change Strategy. In order to affect positive change, the system must enact policies that improve the infrastructure to increase accountability and the capacity of educators to perform in new ways that impact student learning.

Advanced Definitions of the Principal's Role Are Too Limited. The principal as an instructional leader is not a full definition of the role of the principal. It does not encapsulate the moral imperative to make schools great.

> The principal of the future must lead a complex learning organization by helping to establish new cultures in schools that have deep capacities to engage in continuous problem solving and improvement. (p. 28)

Discussion Questions

1. What do you perceive to be barriers to developing the role of the principal as a leader? How can principals overcome these barriers? How can they get those things done?

2. Instead of answering with "if-only" statements, how can you overcome the barriers given what you've got?

3. Talk about some examples of how to "mediate the tensions between local and state forces in a way that gets problems solved."

4. What are some examples of ambiguous messages sent to existing and aspiring principals about the role of the principal in the education system?

5. What are the great things about being a principal?

6. How do your school's (district's, state's) policies affect student learning? Select one particular policy in effect at your school and discuss its connection to student learning. If it cannot be connected to student learning, what can you do to help it connect or get the policy changed?

7. What does the principal of the future look like? Discuss the emerging picture of the principal as chief operating officer.

8. What lever is powerful enough to usher in a new era of system reform?

Activities

● *If Only I Had . . .*

Time: 20 minutes

Materials: Chart paper, markers

Organize participants into small groups of three or four. Ask them to brainstorm a list of all the if-onlys they can think of. For example, if only we had a paraprofessional for every classroom, then we could meet every student's needs. Have them write their lists on chart paper or other large paper.

On a second sheet of paper have the groups reword the statements to include sentences that begin with "I (or we) can have . . ." For example, we can have a teacher aide in every classroom, then we can meet every student's needs.

Finally, encourage the groups to discuss how they can realize their goals. By changing the wording, the emphasis shifts to action. Challenge participants to think about what they can DO to make it happen, instead of placing blame elsewhere.

● *The Responsibility Virus*

Time: 30 minutes (45 minutes, with reading)

Materials: Chart paper, markers, *The Moral Imperative of School Leadership* by Michael Fullan

Organize participants into small groups of three or four. Give each group chart paper and markers.

If they haven't already read the section on "The Responsibility Virus," ask the participants to read it (pp. 20-21). Encourage them to discuss the significance of the virus on the performance of the principal. If they feel comfortable doing so, ask them to share their feelings about their own "virus."

Instruct the groups to make a visual representation of the responsibility virus and share their work with the large group. It could take the form of an illustration, a chart, a cartoon, or anything else the group desires. Invite participants to share their work and their perceptions about how the responsibility virus affects them.

● *What Doesn't Work*

Time: 15 minutes

Materials: Paper, pens, wastebasket, *The Moral Imperative of School Leadership* by Michael Fullan

Instruct participants to read the section on system-imposed barriers, especially the subheading "Centralization/Decentralization" (pp. 21-22).

Invite participants to make a list of what doesn't work to affect positive change in the public education system. Allow a few minutes for people to write, but beware the lists could get long. Now have the participants wad up the papers and throw them into the wastebasket.

Guide a discussion about what WILL work to affect positive change in the public education system.

● *Help Wanted*

Time: 20–30 minutes

Materials: Paper, pens

Invite participants to write a help-wanted advertisement for the job of modern principal. Encourage them to think about the ideal role of the principal as chief operating officer rather than the current job description.

Request volunteers to share their ads within small groups. If they desire, groups can share their best work with the large group. How can school leaders use these ideas to raise awareness about the new role of the principal?

Journal Writing

How do my perceptions of the system limit my actions? Give some concrete examples of events that might have been influenced by your perceptions.

Practical Application

Before adjourning the session, invite each person to describe the distribution of leadership at his or her school and the function of each level. This would include department heads, special counsels, leadership teams, etc.

Ask each participant to create a leadership roster for his or her school. How is leadership distributed at the school? It might take the form of a pyramid, a tree, or a grid. Whatever the shape, the roster should clearly show the various leadership roles at the school and who fills them. A job description for each position would further clarify the roles.

At the next session, facilitate a discussion among the participants to help them analyze their leadership distribution. Have participants form partners or triads and assist each other with the analysis. Encourage participants to evaluate how they interact with and influence each level.

Chapter 3: The Moral Imperative at the School Level

- "Moral purpose of the highest order is having a system where all students learn, the gap between high and low performance becomes greatly reduced, and what people learn enables them to be successful citizens and workers in a morally based knowledge society." (p. 29)

- The new role of principal should be driven by "moral purpose and all other capacities should be in the service of moral purpose." (p. 30)

- Figure 3.1 (p. 30) displays a hierarchy of moral purpose. In order to make a difference in society, leaders must encompass all four levels of the hierarchy.

- Chapter 3 focuses on the moral imperative of the principals in their schools and communities.

Level 1: Individual

Many school leaders are committed to making a difference in the lives of individual students or teachers. This is admirable, but will not affect widespread change in the system.

Level 2: School

In the current climate, school change occurs at various levels of depth. Chapter 3 presents examples of three levels of depth—surface, 25%, and 50%—through case studies of several schools.

At the surface level, two principals emerged with what seemed to be strong moral imperative. Their proposals sounded good, and programs were begun to achieve their goals, yet when opposition surfaced, the principals retreated or failed to follow through. To dig to the deeper levels, a principal must establish relational trust, be consistent, and have integrity. Change at the school level can only occur when the principal creates a safe, trusting, supportive, stable environment.

At the 25% level, one school district implemented a plan to improve literacy using a quality literacy program, providing intense professional development, and providing ongoing feedback and evaluation. As part of the professional development piece, instructional leaders were given professional development opportunities in leadership and literacy. In addition, principals and assistant principals were given monthly opportunities for professional development to strengthen leadership skills.

At the 50% level, one school established an evidence-based approach to school improvement. The principal led staff members in assessing data as a basis for decision-making. In another example, a courageous principal, through persistence and persuasion, formed a faculty that "collaborated in instructional changes, assessment, and student results and made connections toward and facilitated interaction with parents." (p. 37)

In several other case studies, principals reached the 50% level by focusing on: teacher development, teacher leadership, supporting professional learning communities, immediately addressing problems and taking opportunities to reinforce school values. Most important, school leaders selected the right people and worked to develop and support them.

- *The Emerging Image of the Moral Imperative of the Principalship.* The principal plays a vital role in developing and sustaining relational trust in the school. Solid relational trust reaps many rewards. Schools with strong trust relationships are more likely to be among those improving over time. Strong relational trust will ultimately affect student achievement because it reduces vulnerability in new situations, facilitates problem solving, strengthens the professional community, and creates a moral resource for school improvement.

Four important traits characterize successful schools and principals: respect, competence, personal regard for others, and integrity. If all four of these traits are embedded in the school culture, the organization will have a strong culture of discipline and school improvement can begin.

- "The point of this chapter is that leading schools . . . requires principals with the courage and capacity to build new cultures based on trusting relationships and a culture of disciplined inquiry and action. . . . Leading schools through complex reform agendas requires new leadership that goes far beyond improving test scores." (p. 45)

Discussion Questions

1. What is the moral imperative of principals within their schools?

2. "What could be more powerful than to marry moral purpose and additional means to act on it?" (p. 40). What would you do with more resources to actualize your moral imperative?

3. What data is available for you and your staff to use as a tool for school improvement? What do you do with that data? If no data is available, what can you and your colleagues devise as evidence to measure change?

4. How can principals and other school leaders help policymakers realize the depth and breadth of change required in the role of principal to support fundamental change in the system?

5. What is the difference between the "leader as disciplinarian and the culture of discipline?" Which is more effective for sustained development in a school system?

Activities

● *Jigsaw Reading and Discussion*

Time: 45 minutes

Materials: A visual of Levels of the Moral Imperative (p. 30), paper, pens, *The Moral Imperative of School Leadership* by Michael Fullan

Before beginning the activity, display Figure 3.1 so everyone can see the four levels of moral imperative. Pose a question to activate thinking. For example, ask participants to determine what level they think they are currently on based on what they already know about the four levels. If time allows ask participants to write their responses on notepaper or in a journal. Have volunteers share their thoughts aloud.

Organize participants into small groups. Group size will depend on the number of participants in your workshop.

Assign each group one portion of the section "Level 2: Making a Difference in the School." (p. 31). For example, assign each group one case study to read. Encourage the groups to read the selection together and then discuss the main idea. They should prepare a statement about their selection to share with the large group. Allow about 10–15 minutes for groups to read and discuss, then call the large group back together. Invite a representative from each group to review the main idea of the selection they read.

After all groups have had a chance to share their summaries, guide a discussion about the significance of the case studies. Ask questions that elicit descriptions of what school leaders at each level look like and can achieve.

● *Relational Trust*

Time: 30 Minutes

Materials: Chart paper, markers, masking tape

Organize participants into pairs or small groups. Give each group chart paper and markers.

Invite participants to divide the chart paper in half and label the left side *Trust Building,* and the right side *Trust Destroying.* Ask groups to write down words, actions, policies, or behaviors that build trust among a school staff or destroy trust among a staff.

Have groups post their chart paper on the walls around the room. Give volunteers ample opportunity to share their thoughts with the large group.

Journal Writing

Evaluate the level of data-based inquiry at your school. What can you do to lead the process to improve?

Evaluate the level of disciplined action at your school. How will you facilitate its improvement?

Evaluate the level of trust in your school. How can it improve?

Practical Application

Organize your current school leaders (or create a team) to complete a data-based inquiry task at your school site.

What will they study? What evidence will be used? What is the expected outcome? How will this inquiry improve student achievement?

Record your actions and progress in your journal to share with your peers.

Chapter 4: Making a Difference Beyond the School

- School leaders are morally responsible for changing the context in all schools, not just their own. Principals are in a unique position to collaborate with their counterparts in other schools, districts, and even countries to improve the system and help students achieve.

- For large numbers of schools and communities to operate with moral purpose, individual school principals must make a commitment to success for all schools in the district. When school leaders are committed to widespread change, the system will follow because of the inherent discipline and accountability in the principals' actions.

- Principals must be acutely aware of the state of public education in society. Principals must be aware of the bigger picture and incorporate it into daily leadership.

Level 3: Making a Difference Regionally

For deep and lasting change, reform must reach all schools in the district.

Districtwide change can occur a various levels of depth. Chapter 4 presents examples of two levels of depth—25%, and 50%—through case studies of several districts.

An example of a district at the 25% level: At a district in Baltimore, school leaders theoretically learned from one another during monthly meetings. Two days each month were devoted to professional development for school leaders and principals. One day was devoted to literacy and the second for leadership practices.

An example of a district at the 50% level: District 2 in New York City demonstrated dramatic improvements in reading and math. This success is partially attributed to monthly meetings by the principals to develop and build the "shared professional point of view of the district" (Fink & Resnick, 2001, p. 601).

The role of the district is critical to widespread improvement. "Without the district, reform across many schools will not happen" (p. 55). Yet, it is easy to lose sight of the critical role of the principal. Districts must be careful not to implement "informed external prescription," but rather to facilitate "cultural change and relational trust" that will engage passionate and dedicated educators in the fight for sustained reform. When the pressure to reform comes from external sources, school leaders and principals inevitably feel the strain. Educators must be compelled to facilitate reform by an intrinsic moral purpose.

"If we accept that all our futures depend on the quality of education for all children, then we all have a vested interest in raising standards across the board, not only in our own institutions" (Miliband, 2002b, p. 5). School leaders with a strong moral imperative will share what they know with others and learn from each other. The role of the principal must change. The principal must focus capacity and resources on improving student achievement in his or her own school and beyond.

Level 4: School Leadership and Society

School leaders must study and appreciate the value of key state policies, performance evidence, and student achievement studies. They must be aware of the larger context and how it affects their individual school reform.

Effective school leaders will naturally absorb new developments in their interactions with other school leaders. When principals are sharing knowledge and acting across all levels of society they will be infused with knowledge of state policies, new developments in educational reform, and student performance evidence.

Discussion Questions

1. What does it take to achieve districtwide reform?

2. What deep changes would you like to see in your school? In your district? In society?

3. What opportunities do you have to collaborate with and learn from other school leaders in your district? What do you offer

to the other school leaders? What are you doing to facilitate/ support cooperation and collaboration among school leaders in your district?

4. What role does your district play in efforts to reform the system? Can sustained change occur without significant involvement by the district?

5. "Adverse urban conditions" are a reality in more and more schools. How do these conditions affect reform? What is the role of the principal in reforming schools with these conditions?

6. What assistance would you like from the district in implementing curriculum changes and leadership training to institute reform? How can you initiate that assistance?

7. How can we make moral purpose worthwhile, energizing, and doable?

Activities

● *Deciding What Works*

Time: 45 minutes

Materials: Note cards, pens

Organize participants into groups of four or five. Give each group a stack of note cards and several pens.

Invite each participant to select three blank note cards and write down three things that are working in their schools or districts to reform the system (one idea per card). Including names and school names should be optional. Allow about 5-7 minutes to write, then have participants place all the completed note cards in the center of the table.

Have the groups review the cards in the center of the table and discuss examples of effective ways to reform the current system. In other words, what is working? Encourage participants to elaborate on what has been discussed. They may draw on personal experiences, insights, or actions, knowledge about particular practices, key pieces of legislation, or thoughts about student performance indicators. Invite participants to jot down key points from their discussion to share with the large group.

Ask volunteers to share their ideas with the large group. Start a discussion about what is working for various schools and districts. Guide the discussion to expand on what they can do to support each other in the quest to achieve significant, sustained reform.

● *The Big Picture*

Time: 15 minutes

Materials: Poster paper, markers

Draw an outline of a television screen or a movie screen on poster paper. Label it *The Big Picture*.

Start a discussion about the last section of Chapter 4—Level 4: School Leadership and Society. Guide the discussion around the idea of seeing the big picture. Educators must be aware of state policies, student performance indicators, and achievement studies when embarking on the quest for education reform. Many educators may not know where to find information to stay in touch.

Invite participants to help you make a list of places they can acquire information to keep themselves current about policies and achievement indicators. Pose questions that get participants thinking about where they find information—professional journals, standardized testing reports, government Web sites, etc. Write all the sources in the frame of *The Big Picture*.

Encourage participants to record the names of the resources they might wish to refer to in the future.

Journal Writing

What are the key educational issues at the provincial or state levels? At the federal or national levels? How does my knowledge of these policies affect daily interactions at my school?

Practical Application

Reach out to a fellow principal or school leader at another school in your district. Arrange a regular meeting time and agenda. Can you include any more leaders in your meetings?

How can you collaborate to improve the achievement at all schools? What knowledge can you share with others in the group? What can you learn from others?

Record your actions and progress in your journal to share with your peers.

Chapter 5: How to Get There: The Individual and the System

- Avoid getting bogged down in the extrinsic prescription, or "tell me how to do it." The moral imperative has no extrinsic road map for how to get there, simply guidelines and suggestions.

However, individual and system action are both required for system reform. Individuals cannot wait for the system to get reform started and the system must create and support change.

The Individual

- As school leaders, individuals take risks when acting on the moral imperative. Principals must take action to implement change. In order to affect significant change, principals must establish a climate of relationship trust. When pushing for school reform, school leaders must compel others to buy into their vision for change. Principals foster support for this vision when they respect and affirm teachers, exhibit integrity, and competently manage every day affairs. By placing trust in worthy teachers who collectively support a common reform agenda, principals can begin the hard work of school improvement.

- When developing a reciprocal trust relationship, Reina and Reina (1999) suggest three types of trust to be actively developed by leaders:

  Competence Trust

  Contractual Trust

  Communication Trust

- Another way school leaders can foster development of colleagues is by "letting go and reining in." Give teachers the opportunity to learn, trust that they will fulfill their responsibilities, and provide a supportive environment for risk-taking and problem solving. A natural system of checks and balances, accountability and performance, is built in to regular and consistent interaction among peers.

- School leaders must avoid overresponsibility and underresponsibility by embracing new governing values, including:

  Informed choice versus "win, don't lose"

  Internal commitment versus maintaining control

  Open testing versus avoiding embarrassment

  Being authentic versus staying rational (Martin, 2002)

- Instead of striving for high-profile, charismatic leadership qualities, the "new" principal displays restraint, modesty, intensity (Badaracco, 2002), innocence, curiosity, capacity (Heifetz & Linsky, 2002), personal humility and professional will (Collins, 2001).

- School districts are taking some steps toward advancing the role of school leaders. Principals must push the envelope for changing the context.

The System

- For moral purpose to thrive, we must transform leadership in the school system.

  1. Reconceptualize the role of school leadership

     Redefine the principal as chief operating officer

     Give the principal greater authority

     Give principals more money and more discretion over spending

     Attract leaders by providing more resources

     See that principals operate at all four levels of the moral imperative

  2. Recognize and work with the continuum of development

     Organize the system so you can start on the continuum of development

     Focus on the long-term goal of decentralization

  3. Get school size right

     Smaller schools make it easier to develop morally driven cultures

     Smaller schools provide more opportunity to interact with other school leaders in the district

  4. Invest in leaders developing leaders

     The success of a leader is determined by how many good leaders are left behind

     They system must provide resources and opportunities for leaders from different schools to learn from each other

     Develop the leadership skills on all levels—not just the principalship

  5. Improve the teaching profession

     Improve the individual development and performance of teachers

     Improve the working conditions of teachers

     Reducing the poor performance of some teachers will help develop a culture of self-discipline

  6. Improve the capacity of the infrastructure

     Facilitate leadership through state policy and programs

     Improve working conditions

     Provide new resources

     Insist on competent teachers

Discussion Questions

1. After reading Chapters 1 through 4, everything sounds wonderful. Yes, we need to change the role of principals. Yes, we need to change the system and change must be guided by the moral imperative. So, now, the natural question is, "How do we do that?" Why do you think Fullan does not give an explicit, step-by-step guide for how to accomplish these tasks?

2. How does an effective leader deal with teachers who do not warrant trust?

3. What strategies can be used to help others cope with the tension associated with change?

4. How do the individual and the system work together to create meaningful, sustained change in the public education system?

5. How would you redefine the role of the principal?

6. What must be present to move from performance training sects to professional learning communities? (p. 74)

7. Given the current climate, is there any feasible way to get school size right?

8. What programs are in place to allow leaders to earn from other leaders?

9. How do poor performing teachers affect a school climate? What can be done to reduce their effect on school climate if they cannot be convinced to change their ways or counseled out of the profession?

10. In what way can independent facilities or government agencies support leadership development?

Activities

● *Individuals Can Make a Difference*

Time: 30 minutes

Materials: "Sticky" notes, pens, chart paper, markers, masking tape

"Get the right people on board, confront the brutal facts, and establish a culture of discipline in which doing the right thing is built into the culture, combine deep personal humility with intense professional will . . ." (p. 64).

Give participants stacks of "sticky" notes and pens. Post four sheets of chart paper on the walls around the room. Label each of the four sheets with one of the following titles:

Get the Right People on Board

Confront the Brutal Facts

Establish a Culture of Discipline

Combine Deep Personal Humility With Intense Professional Will

Ask participants to help their colleagues figure out how to achieve these difficult tasks. Have participants write down their thoughts, insights, and advice on the "sticky" notes, then place them on the chart paper with the corresponding title.

After a few minutes, ask the participants to regroup. Invite a volunteer near each poster to read the comments on the chart paper. As he or she is reading, pause and generate a discussion about the proposed ideas. Ask participants to think about how they can learn to improve in these areas and incorporate the new ideas offered during this session.

● **Trust**

Time: 30 minutes

Materials: Paper, pens, *The Moral Imperative of School Leadership* by Michael Fullan

Developing and maintaining trust is a difficult thing to accomplish. It is a reciprocal proposition that must involve both parties. Reina and Reina (1999) have defined three components of trust that must be actively reinforced by school leaders—competence trust, contractual trust, communication trust.

Ask participants to refer to Reina and Reina's list of components of trust on page 66. Have them write the subcomponents on a sheet of paper and then give an example of an everyday occurrence that fosters trust.

Example: Respect people's judgment—accept all propositions during a faculty meeting, listen carefully to all propositions, and consider all options with equal care

Allow about 10 minutes for participants to write, then invite them share their thoughts with a partner or in a small group. Finally, ask volunteers to share with the large group.

Leadership Is Risky Business

Time: 10 minutes

Materials: Chart paper, markers

> Exercising leadership can get you into a lot of trouble. (Heifetz & Linsky, 2002)

Write the quote on chart paper for everyone to see. Read it aloud and give participants some time to think about the words.

Invite participants to brainstorm some things that might never have happened if someone had not had the courage to take a risk. For example, Martin Luther King, Jr. took a risk to advance civil rights. Susan B. Anthony took a risk to advance woman suffrage.

Ask participants to discuss a scenario in which school leaders must take a risk. The event could be real or hypothetical. What are the possible benefits of taking the risk? What would happen if no risk were taken?

I Am an Effective Leader

Time: 30 minutes

Materials: Handout *I Am an Effective Leader* (see page 23 of facilitator's guide), butcher paper, markers, pens

Organize participants into small groups. Cover the table in butcher paper and place some markers in the middle of the table. Ask participants to brainstorm all the characteristics and actions of an effective leader and write their thoughts on the table so everyone can see. Allow a few minutes for groups to discuss their thoughts.

Give participants a copy of the *I Am an Effective Leader* handout and pens or pencils. Ask them to complete the statements with words and phrases that describe the characteristics and actions of an effective leader. Encourage participants to keep their papers and refer to them as they continue on their moral journey.

Revamping the System

Time: 30 minutes

Materials: A visual of Strategic Directions for Transforming Leadership in School Systems (p. 73), *The Moral Imperative of School Leadership* by Michael Fullan

Organize participants into six groups. Assign each group one of the strategic directions listed in Exhibit 5.1 on page 73. Encourage the groups to read the corresponding section in Chapter 5 about the direction they have been assigned and discuss its implications.

Invite a spokesperson from each group to share the key points from the discussion.

Journal Writing

Are the goals set forth in *The Moral Imperative of School Leadership* attainable for the average principal?

What are you doing to fulfill the moral imperative to improve society?

School leadership is being redefined. How would you define the new role of the principal in today's school system?

Practical Application

Make a firm commitment to work toward instituting at least one of the strategies discussed in *The Moral Imperative of School Leadership*. Develop a plan of action that will guide your course. Write the plan down and keep it in a place where you will be reminded of it every day. Every day, ask yourself, "Does what I am doing meet the moral imperative?"

I Am an Effective Leader

I am _____

I say _____

I can hear _____

I listen _____

I require _____

I plan to _____

I learn _____

I encourage _____

I support _____

I am proud _____

I am committed to _____

I act _____

I wonder _____

I persevere when _____

I remain quiet _____

I feel _____

I believe _____

I know _____

I value _____

I AM AN EFFECTIVE LEADER.

Sample Workshop Agendas

Half-Day Workshop Agenda

Welcoming Activity (10 minutes)

Purpose of Workshop (5 minutes)

- Examine the qualities of a successful leader and determine the moral imperative of school leaders.
- Recognize the barriers to school reform and identify ways to change current thinking in order to change the context in which you work.
- Understand the Levels of the Moral Imperative.
- Explore how school leaders create meaningful, sustained change.
- Engage in professional interaction.
- Explore the role of principals and other school leaders in reform.
- Reflect on personal practices and perceptions.

Chapter 1 (1 hour)

1. Discuss the qualities of the Level 5 Leader
2. Activity: "Acting as a Level 5 Leader"

Chapter 2 (45 minutes)

1. Barriers to School Leadership—create charts
2. Activity: "What Doesn't Work"

Break (15 minutes)

Chapter 3 and Chapter 4 (1 hour)

1. Jigsaw activity to discuss the Levels of the Moral Imperative
2. Create a visual of each level
3. Whole group discussion

Chapter 5 (30 minutes)

1. Small group discussion of question "How do the individual and the system work together to create meaningful, sustained change in the public education system?"
2. Large group sharing, connect to summary

Summary and Evaluation (20 minutes)

One-Day Workshop Agenda

Welcoming Activity (10 minutes)

Purpose of Workshop (5 minutes)

- Examine the qualities of a successful leader and determine the moral imperative of school leaders.
- Recognize the barriers to school reform and identify ways to change current thinking in order to change the context in which you work.
- Understand the Levels of the Moral Imperative.
- Explore how school leaders create meaningful, sustained change.
- Engage in professional interaction.
- Explore the role of principals and other school leaders in reform.
- Reflect on personal practices and perceptions.

Chapter 1

1. Activity: "Informed Professional Judgment" (30 minutes)
2. Discuss the qualities of the Level 5 Leader (15 minutes)
3. Activity: "Acting as a Level 5 Leader" (1 hour)

Break (15 minutes)

Chapter 2 (45 minutes)

1. Barriers to School Leadership—create charts
2. Activity: "What Doesn't Work"

Chapter 3

1. Discussion of the role of principal at the school level (15 minutes)
2. Activity: "Relational Trust" (30 minutes)
3. Discussion of data-based inquiry (15 minutes)

Lunch (1 hour)

Chapter 4

1. Small group discussion question: "What does it take to achieve districtwide reform?" (15 minutes)
2. Activity: "Deciding What Works" (45 minutes)
3. Activity: "The Big Picture" (15 minutes)

Break (15 minutes)

Chapter 5

1. Discussion of the qualities of the "new" principal (15 minutes)
2. Activity: "Individuals Can Make a Difference" (30 minutes)
3. Activity: "Revamping the System" (30 minutes)

Summary and Evaluation (15 minutes)

Two-Day Workshop Agenda

Day One

Welcoming Activity (10 minutes)

Purpose of Workshop (5 minutes)

- Examine the qualities of a successful leader and determine the moral imperative of school leaders.
- Recognize the barriers to school reform and identify ways to change current thinking in order to change the context in which you work.
- Understand the Levels of the Moral Imperative.
- Explore how school leaders create meaningful, sustained change.
- Engage in professional interaction.
- Explore the role of principals and other school leaders in reform.
- Reflect on personal practices and perceptions.

Preface

1. Large group discussion: "What is system transformation? How can principals and other school leaders assist in system transformation? What conditions need to be present to affect powerful change in the system?" (20 minutes)

Chapter 1

1. Small group discussion: "What is the role of public education in society?" (15 minutes)
2. Activity: "Informed Professional Judgment" (30 minutes)
3. Discuss the qualities of the Level 5 Leader (15 minutes)
4. Activity: "Acting as a Level 5 Leader" (1 hour)

Break (15 minutes; insert at appropriate time during Chapter 1)

Activity (1 hour 45 minutes)

Chapter 2

1. Jigsaw of Barriers to School Leadership (45 minutes)
2. Activity: "If Only I Had . . ." (20 minutes)

Lunch (1 hour)

Chapter 2 (continued)

1. Activity: "The Responsibility Virus" (30 minutes)
2. Activity: "What Doesn't Work" (15 minutes)
3. Activity: "Help Wanted" (20 minutes)

Break (15 minutes)

Chapter 3

1. Small group discussion: The limitations of making a difference in the lives of individuals (10 minutes)
2. Large group discussion: "What is the moral imperative of principals within their schools?" (30 minutes)

3. Activity: "Relational Trust" (30 minutes)

4. Discussion of school culture and data-based inquiry (20 minutes)

Day Two

Reconnect activity (15 minutes)

Chapter 4

1. Small group discussion question: Level 3: Making a Difference Regionally (20 minutes)

2. Activity: "Deciding What Works" (45 minutes)

3. Journal writing: Key educational issues (15 minutes)

Break (15 minutes)

Chapter 4 (continued)

4. Small group discussion of key educational issues (15 minutes)

5. Activity: "The Big Picture" (15 minutes)

Chapter 5

1. Small group discussion of new governing values (15 minutes)

2. Discussion of the qualities of the "new" principal (15 minutes)

3. Activity: "Individuals Can Make a Difference" (30 minutes)

4. Large group discussion of trust relationships (10 minutes)

5. Activity: "Trust" (30 minutes)

Lunch (1 hour)

Chapter 5 (continued)

6. Large group discussion: "How does an effective leader deal with teachers who do not warrant trust?" (15 minutes)

7. Activity: "Leadership Is Risky Business" (10 minutes)

8. Activity: "Revamping the System" (30 minutes)

9. Journal writing: How would you define the new role of the principal in today's school system? (15 minutes)

Break (15 minutes)

Chapter 5 (continued):

10. Activity: "I Am an Effective Leader" (30 minutes)

11. Practical application: Plan of action to meet the moral imperative. (30 minutes)

Summary and Evaluation (15 minutes)

Resource A

Professional Development Planning Matrix

Purposes

- Examine the qualities of a successful leader and determine the moral imperative of school leaders.
- Recognize the barriers to school reform and identify ways to change current thinking in order to change the context in which you work.
- Understand the Levels of the Moral Imperative.
- Explore how school leaders create meaningful, sustained change.
- Engage in professional interaction.
- Explore the role of principals and other school leaders in reform.
- Reflect on personal practices and perceptions.

	Preface	Chapter 1	Chapter 2	Chapter 3	Chapter 4	Chapter 5
Half-Day		Discuss the qualities of the Level 5 Leader Activity: "Acting as a Level 5 Leader" Activity: "Acting as a Level 5 Leader"	Barriers to School Leadership—create charts Activity: "What Doesn't Work"	Jigsaw activity to discuss the Levels of the Moral Imperative Create a visual of each level Whole group discussion	Combine with Chapter 3 Jigsaw activities	Small group discussion of question four Large group sharing, connect to summary
One-Day		Activity: "Informed Professional Judgment" Discuss the qualities of the Level 5 Leader Activity: "Acting as a Level 5 Leader"	Barriers to School Leadership—create charts Activity: "What Doesn't Work"	Discussion of the role of principal at the school level Activity: "Relational Trust" Discussion of data-based inquiry	Small group discussion of question one Activity: "Deciding What Works" Activity: "The Big Picture"	Discussion of the qualities of the "new" principal Activity: "Individuals Can Make a Difference" Activity: "Revamping the System"
Two-Day	Large group discussion of questions three, four, and six	Small group discussion of question one Activity: "Informed Professional Judgment"	Jigsaw reading of Barriers to School Leadership Activity: "If Only I Had . . ."	Small group discussion: The limitations of making a difference in the lives of individuals Large group discussion of question one	Small group discussion question: Level 3: Making a Difference regionally Activity: "Deciding What Works"	Small group discussion of new governing values Discussion of the qualities of the "new" principal Activity: "Individuals Can Make a Difference"

(Continued)

Preface	Chapter 1	Chapter 2	Chapter 3	Chapter 4	Chapter 5
	Discuss the qualities of the Level 5 Leader	Activity: The Responsibility Virus"	Large group discussion of question one	Journal writing: Key educational issues	Large group discussion of trust relationships
	Activity: "Acting as a Level 5 Leader"	Activity: "What Doesn't Work"	Activity: "Relational Trust"	Small group discussion of key educational issues	Activity: "Trust"
		Activity: "Help Wanted"	Discussion of school culture and data-based inquiry	Activity: "The Big Picture"	Large group discussion: "How does an effective leader deal with teachers who do not warrant trust?"
					Activity: "Leadership is Risky Business"
					Activity: "Revamping the System"
					Journal writing: How would you define the new role of the principal in today's school system?
					Activity: "I Am an Effective Leader"
					Practical application: Plan of action to meet the moral imperative.

Resource B

Workshop Evaluation Form

Content

How well did the workshop meet the goal and objectives?

How will you apply what you learned during this workshop in your daily professional life?

What professional support will you need to implement what you have learned from this workshop?

How well did the topics explored in this workshop meet a specific need in your school or district?

How relevant was this topic to your professional life?

Process

How well did the instructional techniques and activities facilitate your understanding of the topic?

How can you incorporate the activities learned today into your daily professional life?

Were a variety of learning experiences included in the workshop?

Was any particular activity memorable? What made it stand out?

Context

Were the facilities conducive to learning?

Were the accommodations adequate for the activities involved?

Overall

Overall, how successful would you consider this workshop? Please include a brief comment or explanation.

What was the most valuable thing you gained from this workshop experience?

SOURCE: Adapted from *Evaluating Professional Development* by Thomas R. Guskey, Corwin Press, Inc. 2000.

**CORWIN
PRESS**

The Corwin Press logo—a raven striding across an open book—represents the union of courage and learning. Corwin Press is committed to improving education for all learners by publishing books and other professional development resources for those serving the field of K–12 education. By providing practical, hands-on materials, Corwin Press continues to carry out the promise of its motto: **"Helping Educators Do Their Work Better."**

Printed in the United States
By Bookmasters